LIFE
IN
BIBLE
TIMES

Chris Tarrant
Illustrated by Kim Shaw

Abingdon Press

Nashville

Library of Congress Cataloging-in-Publication Data

Tarrant, Chris.
Life in Bible times.

Includes index.
Summary: Pictures and text depict life in Biblical
times through the stories of ten men and women in
Bible, from Jacob to Paul.
1. Sociology, Biblical—Juvenile literature.
2. Jews—Social life and customers—Juvenile literature.
3. Jews—History—To 70 A.D.—Juvenile literature.
[1. Jews—Social life and customs.   2. Bible stories]
I. Shaw, Kim, ill.   II.Title.
BS670.T27 1985   220.9′5   85–15843

ISBN 0–687–21850–0 (pbk.)

American edition published 1985 by
Abingdon Press, in cooperation with
Scripture Union

Reprinted 1987

Printed in Great Britain

Contents

PEOPLE IN BIBLE TIMES

The Bible is full of stories about real people. We can find out a great deal about them because the writers of the Bible were interested in historical facts. We can also find out about their way of life by looking at remains of houses, statues, weapons, toys and household articles which have been dug up by archaeologists. Other writings such as official records or private letters or bills can supply more details about life at a particular period of history. From all this information we are able to put together pictures of what life was like in Bible times.

Our book covers two thousand years, starting with Jacob, who lived nearly two thousand years before Christ, and ending with Paul, who lived in the first century after the birth of Christ.

God deals with all kinds of men and women in their daily lives. Some Bible stories tell of kings and queens, like Solomon and Esther. More often the stories are about people who would find no place in an ordinary history book – a shepherd, a farmer's wife, or a cloth seller. The countries from which they come are varied too – Israel, Egypt, Persia, Greece and the Roman Empire.

We have been able to choose only ten of the many people in the Bible for this book. There are plenty more for you to discover!

JACOB, a farmer in Palestine

After Isaac and Rebekah were married they had to wait a long time before they had any children. Eventually, they had twins. The first-born was called Esau, or 'Hairy', because he was covered with hair. His brother, Jacob, was born immediately afterwards, and he grew up feeling jealous of Esau. As the elder son, Esau had special privileges. If his father was away, he was in charge of the family and everyone had to obey him. He would inherit his father's property one day.

Like most of his friends, Jacob became a shepherd. He led the family's sheep and goats in search of pasture, returning with them to the camp each evening. Esau preferred the rough and independent life of a hunter, and he pleased his father by giving him meat from any wild animals he killed.

Although he was skillful, there were times when Esau caught nothing on his long hunting trips, and he would return tired and hungry. On one occasion he found Jacob cooking bean soup.

'Let me have some of that,' he said. 'I haven't eaten anything for ages, and I'm famished.'

Jacob realized how desperate Esau was and replied, 'Certainly; but first promise you will give me your birthright.'

'Have whatever you want,' said Esau. 'Just give me some soup quickly.' He did not seem to be worried that he was giving away so much for so little.

Farming in Palestine

Isaac and Rebekah and their family lived with their relations in an encampment. The men were shepherds and pastured their flocks of sheep and goats on the scanty grass and shrubs in the less fertile areas of Palestine. During the long summer drought Isaac and the other herdsmen had

Life in tents

Isaac's sheep and goats provided the family with housing, clothing and food. Rebekah and the other women used the coarse hair of the goats to weave into tent coverings. Jacob and Esau probably helped to put up the tent whenever they moved. The goats'-hair cloth was stretched over the top of three lines of poles and secured by cords to wooden pegs knocked into the ground.

A curtain divided the inside of the tent into rooms. Rebekah used one room for preparing the food. They lived mainly on yogurt and cheese, various soups made from vegetables and bread. Most of the corn for bread-making was bought from the Canaanites, who had built villages in the more fertile areas of the country. Rebekah used a clay oven, shaped like a chimney, to bake the bread.

to travel many miles to find water and pasture. By living in tents they were able to move about more easily. Years later, when Jacob had a family of his own, there was a famine in Palestine. Jacob had to send his sons on a long journey to Egypt to buy the corn they needed.

The other room was used for entertaining. Any stranger arriving at the camp would be invited in and given food and protection.

The family slept on straw mats and spread a piece of leather on the ground for a table. Their clay pots and jars, goatskin bags and lamps could all be carried on a few donkeys.

Once a year Isaac and the other shepherds sheared the sheep. The women spun the wool and made clothing and blankets. It was rare for anyone to have more than two sets of clothing and these would be worn year after year.

MOSES, the spokesman of slaves

To escape from a terrible famine, Jacob had gone with his family and livestock to live in Egypt. A few centuries later, most of his descendants were slaves there, but the upbringing of Moses was very different. He was adopted by an Egyptian princess and brought up in the palace. He was taught by a scribe to read and write, and had plenty of time to play games like leap-frog in the courtyards.

Moses

Moses did not ignore the suffering of his fellow Israelites in slavery. In obedience to God, he went to Pharaoh and asked that they be given three days off work to travel into the desert. There they would offer sacrifices to God.

'You are encouraging the people to be lazy,' replied Pharaoh angrily. 'They will not be allowed to leave their work. Instead they can work harder! In future they can find their own straw to make bricks, and they will continue to make the same number each day.'

Pharaoh

The ancient Egyptians believed in a variety of gods and goddesses. The king of Egypt was thought to be descended from the gods. He was referred to as 'Pharaoh'. No one would presume to call him by his personal name. Moreover, only Pharaoh's sister was considered good enough to become his queen. Anyone who wanted to speak to Pharaoh had to kneel before him. His words then had to be obeyed as though they were from Horus, the god of the sky.

Scribes and writing

Records were kept by skillful scribes who sat cross-legged on the ground and wrote on a roll of papyrus. This was made from the papyrus sedge which grew in marshy areas of the River Nile delta. The stems were cut into thin strips which were hammered together to make a smooth sheet. On a string over his shoulder the scribe carried a case with several reed pens, a water jar, and a palette with cakes of red and black ink.

11

Slave labor

The kings of Egypt relied on the forced labor of many of their subjects, Egyptians as well as foreigners, to complete major building projects such as pyramids, temples and canals. Israelites were used in the building of two cities which were to serve as supply centers. Afraid that the growing number of Israelites might prove a threat to his power, Pharaoh put cruel slave-masters over them. Even the Israelite foremen who organized the work-force were treated harshly, and were often beaten.

Brick making

When straw stubble had been gathered it was trampled into wet clay and then shaped in molds. The bricks were left to bake hard in the sun, and carried up on to wooden scaffolding for the bricklayers. Grain would be stored in the large conical stores made of mud bricks.

At the end of an exhausting day's work the Israelites returned to their rows of one-room huts made of mud, reeds, and wood. Each hut had a flat roof and small holes high up in the walls to allow some light in but keep the heat out. Cooking was done outside. The locally-grown corn produced bread and beer. Vegetables and fruit such as beans, lentils, lettuce, onions, melons, dates and figs were also eaten. Cattle and poultry supplied meat.

DEBORAH, a leader in Israel

As Deborah sat in the shade of a palm tree, her heart went out to the little group of helpless women and children pleading with her. Israelites often came to her for advice and judgments, and went away thankful for her help. However, the threat of Canaanite raids was one that had never been removed.

'Please help us! A group of Canaanites attacked our village last week. Many of our men were killed, and they took all the grain we had stored. For years now they have made us suffer terribly.'

'Lord, your people cannot bear this suffering much longer. They are broken. Show them your great strength and rescue them now.'

The dramatic defeat of the Canaanites which followed was to be a clear sign of God's strength. Deborah ordered Barak to march with a large army to the top of Mount Tabor. When the enemy heard what was happening, they immediately set out with an army. It included nine hundred chariots, enough to rout the poorly-equipped Israelite foot soldiers. However, as Barak moved down the mountainside towards the flat land around the River Kishon there was an unexpected rainstorm. Before long the Canaanite chariot wheels became bogged down in the muddy ground. The river became a raging torrent, and as the Canaanites struggled to escape many of their chariots were washed away. The Israelites chased after the enemy as they fled along the valley, and the victory was so great that peace was restored to the land.

Canaanites and the Promised Land

Moses led the Israelite nation away from slavery in Egypt, across the desert to the borders of the land of Canaan. There Moses died and Joshua became the new leader of the twelve tribes. He led their campaign to claim the land God had promised to give them.

Ambush!

The Canaanites held on to the coastal plain, along which the major land trade routes passed. A century after Joshua's death, Deborah, leader of Israel at the time, was receiving frequent complaints that it was unsafe to travel along the main roads for fear of being robbed by Canaanites. In the coastal ports the produce of farms and forests was loaded into ships which brought back a variety of luxury goods from foreign parts for the wealthy city-dwellers.

Canaanite towns

The walls which surrounded Canaanite towns showed their readiness for battle. The major cities were ruled by kings who were constantly at war with each other in an attempt to increase their own power. This made it easier for Joshua to invade and capture one city after another. When most of the land had been conquered, Joshua divided it between the twelve tribes.

The Promised Land was shared out among the twelve tribes of Israel.

ASHER
DAN
ZEBULUN
NAPHTALI
Mediterranean Sea
ISSACHAR
MANASSEH
MANASSEH
EPHRAIM
GAD
BENJAMIN
DAN Jerusalem
JUDAH
REUBEN
SIMEON

Farming

Most Canaanites were farmers. Some had their own small plots of land, but others were slaves of the wealthy. The long hot and dry summers made farming difficult, but there was a good harvest as long as the rains came at the right time. Unexpected rain storms sometimes occurred in the dry season, as the charioteers discovered when fighting Barak's army.

Canaanite gods

The Israelites did not have the hill country entirely to themselves. Despite the command of God, some Canaanites had been allowed to remain. When the Israelites began to worship the Canaanite gods, God repeatedly used surrounding enemies to bring disaster on his people. It was only when they renewed their commitment to serve him alone that God provided a leader like Deborah or Samson to rescue them. These leaders were known as Judges.

RUTH, a farmer's wife

Family loyalty

During the time of the Judges there was a shortage of food in Israel and many people left. One family settled in Moab but the father and the two sons died. The mother, Naomi, decided to return to Israel. One of her daughters-in-law, Ruth, was very fond of Naomi. She left her home country of Moab to settle in Israel with her. The two women arrived in Bethlehem as poor widows with no one to support them.

The family land

In order to raise some money, Naomi wanted to sell the land she had inherited. Israelites believed all the land was God's and his people held it in trust. If anyone needed to part with his land for a time it remained his right and duty to buy it back as soon as he could afford to. Naomi followed the custom of the day by giving her husband's relatives the first bid for the land.

The family line

Israelites made every effort to ensure that there was a son to continue the family line. If a woman was left childless at her husband's death, it was the responsibility of the man's nearest male relative to marry the widow.

Boaz was not the closest relative, but he wanted to marry Ruth and buy the plot of land. So he met the next-of-kin in the open area beside the gate leading out of Bethlehem. This was the center of town life, where legal business, trade, and social gatherings took place. In front of ten elders, who acted as witnesses, the wish of Boaz was granted. It was then confirmed in a symbolic way when the relative took off a sandal and gave it to Boaz.

Boaz and Ruth were married and had a son named Obed, whose grandson David was to become king of Israel.

Ruth's descendants

Ruth ——— Boaz
Obed
Jesse
David ——— Bathsheba
Solomon

THE BARLEY HARVEST

Gleaning

Ruth and Naomi reached Bethlehem at the beginning of the barley harvest. They needed some grain to make bread, so Ruth walked down past the vineyards to the field that lay below the town. Israelite law forbade a farmer to reap his land right up to the border, or to pick up what was left after the reapers had passed through. This gave poor people like Ruth the chance to pick up, or glean, the remaining grain.

Reaping

The large field was divided into many smaller areas which belonged to different landowners. The plots were separated only by stone boundary markers. Ruth happened to be working in the field of Boaz. When he arrived, Boaz asked his reapers the name of the new girl. Until now he had only heard about her, but he was so impressed by the loyalty she had shown that he treated her generously. Unlike other gleaners, Ruth was given permission to stay close behind the reapers, where most of the grain would be found.

Threshing

After the barley had been cut with a sickle it was bound into sheaves and carried by donkey or by ox cart to the threshing floor. Small amounts, like those collected by Ruth, could be beaten against the ground by hand to free the grain from the stalks. Large harvests were piled two feet deep on the hard clay and trampled on by oxen dragging a wooden sledge which had stones or pieces of iron embedded in its base.

Winnowing

The threshed wheat was tossed up into the air with a wooden fork. The wind blew away the unwanted chaff, while the heavy grain fell straight down. This grain was then sifted to remove any mud or stones. Like others who used the threshing floor, Boaz slept beside his grain at night to protect it from thieves and wild animals.

SOLOMON, a wise king and builder

King David had given the Israelites reason to be proud of their nation. It would not be easy for his successor to earn as much respect and loyalty. Nevertheless, his son, Solomon, longed for the wisdom to govern fairly. It was this, above all else, that he asked the Lord to give him.

The wisdom of Solomon

Reports of Solomon's wisdom spread rapidly. He was famous not only for his wise judgments; he also wrote thousands of proverbs, songs and psalms, and had a deep understanding of nature.

When the Queen of Sheba came from southern Arabia to put Solomon's wisdom to the test, she was speechless at all she heard and saw in his magnificent palace. The king could easily answer all of her questions and riddles, and his wealth was evident even in the feasts he provided. On an ordinary day he slaughtered thirty cows and a hundred sheep to feed his household, and silver cups were considered too cheap to be used in the palace. Only gold was good enough.

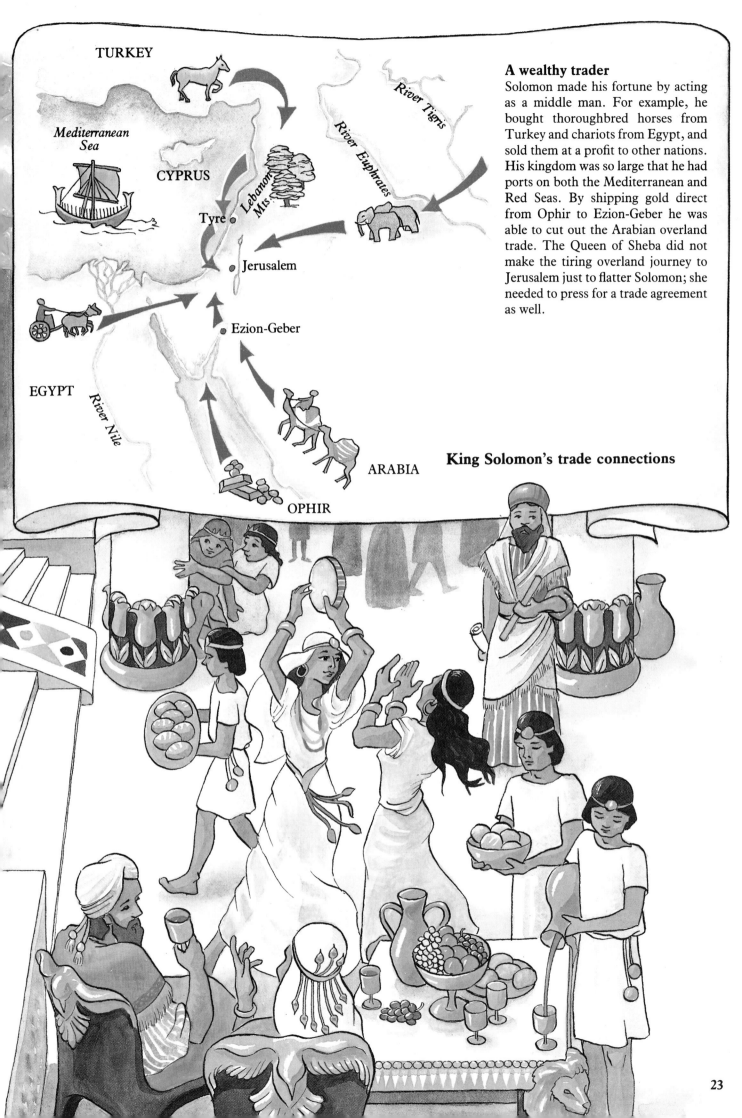

TURKEY

Mediterranean Sea

CYPRUS

River Tigris

River Euphrates

Lebanon Mts.

Tyre

Jerusalem

Ezion-Geber

EGYPT

River Nile

ARABIA

OPHIR

A wealthy trader

Solomon made his fortune by acting as a middle man. For example, he bought thoroughbred horses from Turkey and chariots from Egypt, and sold them at a profit to other nations. His kingdom was so large that he had ports on both the Mediterranean and Red Seas. By shipping gold direct from Ophir to Ezion-Geber he was able to cut out the Arabian overland trade. The Queen of Sheba did not make the tiring overland journey to Jerusalem just to flatter Solomon; she needed to press for a trade agreement as well.

King Solomon's trade connections

The ark

The ark of the covenant was much more important than its size might suggest. Not only did it contain the tablets of the law given to Moses; it also served as the earthly throne of the Lord. The gold-coated box was kept out of sight of the people in a windowless room, and at either end was a carved creature with wings outstretched, as though on guard.

Stone

In local limestone quarries huge blocks were loosened by driving wooden wedges into the cracks and soaking them with water until they expanded. The stones were then cut and shaped in the quarries to avoid unnecessary noise on the holy building site. So skillfully were they prepared and laid that no cement was needed.

Solomon's temple

A church is the meeting house where God's people join today in worship. Solomon's temple served a different purpose; it was to be the earthly home of God himself. Only the religious officials went into the temple building; others worshipped and offered sacrifices in the temple courts.

The cedars of Lebanon

The inside of the temple was lined with planks of cedar and pine, and with beautiful wooden carvings decorated with gold. The timber had to be brought from the distant highlands of Lebanon. The logs were tied together and floated down the coast before being dragged inland by oxen.

The altar

Happy at the birth of a baby? Sorry for a wrong action? Fulfilling a vow? These were some of the occasions on which animals or birds were taken to the temple court to be sacrificed on the tall altar. The smell of roast flesh hung in the air. Sheep bleated as they were held firmly for inspection by the priests; only the best would do.

JEREMIAH, defender of the faith

The glory of Solomon's empire did not last long. Civil war resulted in two separate kingdoms being formed, Israel and Judah. Neither could defend itself successfully against the growing strength of surrounding nations. A century after the conquest of the northern kingdom, Israel, Jeremiah became a prophet in the small southern kingdom of Judah. The Babylonian empire was expanding rapidly and the people of Judah lived in fear for their lives.

Sun worship

Jeremiah was very angry that the Israelites did not turn to God in their trouble. Jerusalem was full of idols, and the religious leaders encouraged worship of foreign gods in the Temple courts. At dawn people could be seen in front of the altar with their backs to the Temple, worshipping the rising sun as though it were a god.

God's messengers

God repeatedly sent messages to his people through his prophets. Jeremiah gave them a final warning to abandon idol worship and put their trust in God alone. Their way of life must reflect the love and justice God demanded of them. If they failed to respond, God would use the Babylonian army to punish them.

Jeremiah and the ox-yoke

Jeremiah often used examples of everyday things to make his meaning clear. After the first defeat of Judah, the Babylonians took the king and other leading Israelites into exile. Jeremiah put a wooden ox-yoke round his neck and warned the people, 'You also will serve the enemy like yoked oxen which have to do what the farmer wants.'

God's prophets were often hated. Jeremiah was laughed at, ignored, and even thrown into prison. There were others who called themselves prophets, but they made up messages that would keep people happy. One of these false prophets tore the yoke off Jeremiah, and told the people that the enemy would soon be defeated. It was not long before the truth was known.

The siege of Jerusalem

When the Babylonians took the king of Judah into exile they appointed a weak ruler called Zedekiah to replace him. Jeremiah warned Zedekiah not to rebel, but the officials and false prophets persuaded the king that victory was in sight. The Babylonians soon marched to Judah, determined to destroy the nation completely. Most of the towns were captured easily. Then Jerusalem itself was surrounded and besieged.

Although Jerusalem had a source of water inside its massive walls, there were limited stores of food. As the siege dragged on food rations began to run out, and many starved to death.

Babylonian attackers

The Babylonian army used local timber to make siege engines. Archers shot at the defenders from the advancing platform, while soldiers were protected from enemy fire as they slammed the battering ram against the walls. Where necessary a mound was built up against the wall first, and the engine was pushed up a log track. At a safer distance, lines of shields protected archers as they took aim.

Israelite defenders

Meanwhile, from the parapets and wooden galleries on the walls the Israelites hurled stones, blazing torches and boiling oil on any who came within range. They also used slings and bows to reach the enemy archers.

Destruction of Jerusalem

After eighteen months, the wall was damaged sufficiently for the enemy to stream over on scaling ladders and make a passage for the cavalry to enter. The city was set on fire and a terrible slaughter followed. The temple and other important buildings were destroyed, and the walls were flattened. Anything of value was taken to Babylon, along with most of the Israelite survivors. Only the poorest people were left to farm the land. Jeremiah was among those allowed to stay.

ESTHER,
a brave queen of Persia

'I will have some of that perfume on my hair, please, and more eyeshadow.' Queen Esther wanted to be at her most attractive in her royal gown because she was about to put her life at risk. The king had issued a decree from his palace in Susa that all of the exiles from Judah should be slaughtered on a set day. Esther had never told him that she was Jewish, and she was about to try to save her fellow Jews. However, Persian kings took great pride in their power, and even wives were not allowed into their presence unless they were called for. Queen Esther had not seen her husband for the last month.

Esther walked through the palace garden with its exotic plants on her way from the women's living quarters, called the harem. She entered the inner courtyard which faced the throne room, being careful not to step on the purple carpet reserved for the king's use.

'What is your request, Queen Esther?' asked the king. He held out the gold scepter, as a sign that her life was spared. She walked across the large throne room with its many high decorated columns. Kneeling before the king, she touched the tip of the scepter.

'Please will you and your prime minister come tonight to a special feast I am preparing for you? Then I will tell you.'

Esther's courage was rewarded. The Jewish people were allowed to go on living thoughout the Persian empire.

Life in exile

After the Persians had overrun the Babylonian empire, exiles from Judah were allowed to return home. However, many had begun to prosper and preferred to stay in Persia. Although Esther's rise to fame was due to an unusual type of beauty contest, other Jews had become influential by normal means. Royal princes were among the customers of one largely Jewish banking house, which lent money at high rates of interest and helped in the complex task of collecting taxes.

The Royal Road

Other Jews became traders, and sometimes travelled along the Royal Road. This road stretched from Susa to the western limit of the empire, and it took camel caravans ninety days to travel along it. At various points there were guard posts, and tolls had to be paid by those travelling along it. The road enabled the king to get news of what was happening in his empire, although even the most urgent message took a week to be carried from the borders by messengers on horseback.

Farming in Persia

Many Jews settled in the fertile lands bordering the Tigris and Euphrates Rivers, and worked as peasant farmers for wealthy landlords. Lack of rainfall made irrigation of the rich black soil essential. The Persians were experts at building irrigation canals, and they raised water to field level in a variety of ways. They invented a water wheel which could use ox-power to irrigate much larger areas than the traditional shaduf – a bucket on one end of a pole with a counterweight on the other end.

Large harvests of wheat and barley could be expected each year, and date palms were grown widely. The palms were heavily taxed because they provided not only food, wine and honey, but also raw materials for making rope and baskets. As the empire expanded, crops such as rice and flax were successfully introduced from other parts.

JESUS, teacher and healer

The attendant carefully picked the scroll out of the ark, removed the embroidered cover, and gave it to Jesus. There was complete silence as Jesus walked to the reader's platform, unrolled the scriptures, and read from the Prophets. In front of him were several rows of men wearing talliths covering their heads. In the gallery were the women and children, forbidden to do any more than watch the service. Behind him sat the President of the synagogue and the most important men in the community. Many of them were Pharisees, and Jesus knew that in their jealousy they were trying to catch him out. Their chance came when Jesus told a man with a deformed hand to stand up in front of everyone.

In their concern to keep God's law, the Pharisees had tried to apply it to every possible situation. For example, work was forbidden on the Sabbath, but what counted as work? The Pharisees thought that healing was work, so they now waited eagerly to see what Jesus would do. They were horrified when Jesus turned to them and asked, 'What does your law allow us to do on the Sabbath? To help or harm, to save life or kill?'

The Pharisees could not give an answer. Jesus then told the man to stretch out his hand, and it was restored. The Pharisees were furious, and met afterwards to plan how they might kill Jesus.

Although used for worship on the Sabbath, the synagogue served as a school, a courtroom and a meeting hall on other days of the week.

A movable ark containing the hand-written scriptures was kept behind curtains at the front of every synagogue. It was an imitation of the original ark of the covenant, lost centuries before. In front of the ark a lamp was kept alight permanently as a sign of God's unfailing presence.

The Temple in Jerusalem

For many Jews the local synagogue was a poor substitute for worship in the Temple in Jerusalem. Only there could sacrifices be offered, and during the three main annual festivals Jerusalem was thronged with pilgrims from distant lands. The Temple was a magnificent new building, constructed at the orders of King Herod. Sadly, some of the priests were corrupt and used their positions to become the wealthiest people in the city.

Pharisees

They were very strict about praying and keeping God's law. Some were very proud of their religion and showed off by wearing oversize phylacteries on their forehead and left arm. These small boxes of black leather contained four scripture passages on tiny pieces of parchment.

Some Pharisees prayed aloud on street corners, hoping to be noticed and admired. Jesus was angry with their sham.

Passover festival

A few days before the great Passover festival, sheep for sacrifice were seen being herded through the streets towards the Temple. The Passover celebration was an annual reminder of how God had brought the Israelites out of slavery in Egypt during Moses' lifetime.

Roman soldiers

It was not surprising that the Jews hated the Romans so much. They had to pay them taxes and Roman soldiers could order people to do things for them. For example, a Jew might be forced to carry a heavy load of grain to the soldiers' barracks. Pontius Pilate was Roman governor in Jesus' lifetime and it was he who had Jesus crucified to please the Jewish leaders. He was especially keen to avoid trouble during the Passover festival when so many Jews were in the city.

LYDIA, a Greek cloth merchant

'Too expensive? Sir, this cloth has been dyed with the juice of the best shellfish on the Mediterranean shores. The Emperor himself would be pleased to wear such a fine shade of purple.'

The wealthy Romans in Philippi wore out Lydia with their fierce bargaining. She was glad that tomorrow she would have a day off. As usual on the Sabbath, she would meet up with some other women to go through the Jewish service of prayer. Although she was not a Jew herself, she was attracted by their faith in a single God who actively cared for his people.

A riverside meeting

While Lydia and the other women were sitting beside the river outside the town, a group of men joined them. After they had introduced themselves as believers in the same God, one of them, called Paul, explained the truth about Jesus. Lydia had occasionally heard the Jews talk about Jesus, but she could never understand why they hated all he stood for. Now she could see the reason and, unlike those Jews, she believed that he was indeed the Savior whom God had promised to send. She would never forget the joy of that day when she waded into the river with the rest of her household to be baptized. Nor would Paul forget the event, for Lydia was the first convert to Christianity in Europe.

Paul, the letter writer

A few years later Paul was in prison because of violent opposition to his preaching. However he was encouraged to know that there were now many Christians in Philippi, and he asked a fellow Christian to take a letter to them. He thanked them for the gift of money they had sent, and urged them, 'Stand firm together and make sure that your way of life matches up to what Jesus demands of you.'

Philippi, a Roman colony

Two men were standing in the middle of the wide forum of Philippi watching laden wagons passing along the Egnatian Way. They were dressed in togas trimmed with purple, and were speaking Latin.

'It is a shame that those wagons are not carrying gold. I gather that when Alexander the Great's father built this city four hundred years ago he used the gold from the local mines to keep his army happy and to offer bribes. He might have left some for us!'

'Yes, and Philip knew where to build cities too. No wonder he named this town after himself. Just thirteen miles inland and guarding the main west-east route through this line of hills, I am not surprised it has now been given the privileged status of 'Roman colony'. The emperor can use us to sort out any trouble in the area, and he can bring in more troops easily enough. I miss Rome, but at least we don't have to speak the language of the locals or follow their strange customs.'

While they were talking, a group of slaves was herded through the forum. The two men looked to see if any might be worth buying at the auction. They could well afford to have a few more, even though recently they had both been persuaded to buy some of Lydia's most expensive cloth.

PAUL, traveller across the Roman Empire

For more than five centuries the Romans ruled over an Empire that stretched from Egypt in the south to Britain in the north. It was not easy to control, as there were many different groups of people who had their own languages and beliefs. So the Romans built straight roads to link every border with Rome. This made it possible to move soldiers and supplies quickly to deal with any rebellion. The roads were well constructed of layers of sand and crushed stone, with concrete and blocks of stone on top. Paul often travelled along these roads on his long missionary journeys.

Roman towns were important centers of trade and administration. The busy market place was surrounded by graceful public buildings with decorated stone columns and arches. There were also temples to the many gods worshipped by the Romans. When they were not working, the townspeople liked to visit the public baths or see the gladiator fights and chariot-racing in the stadium.

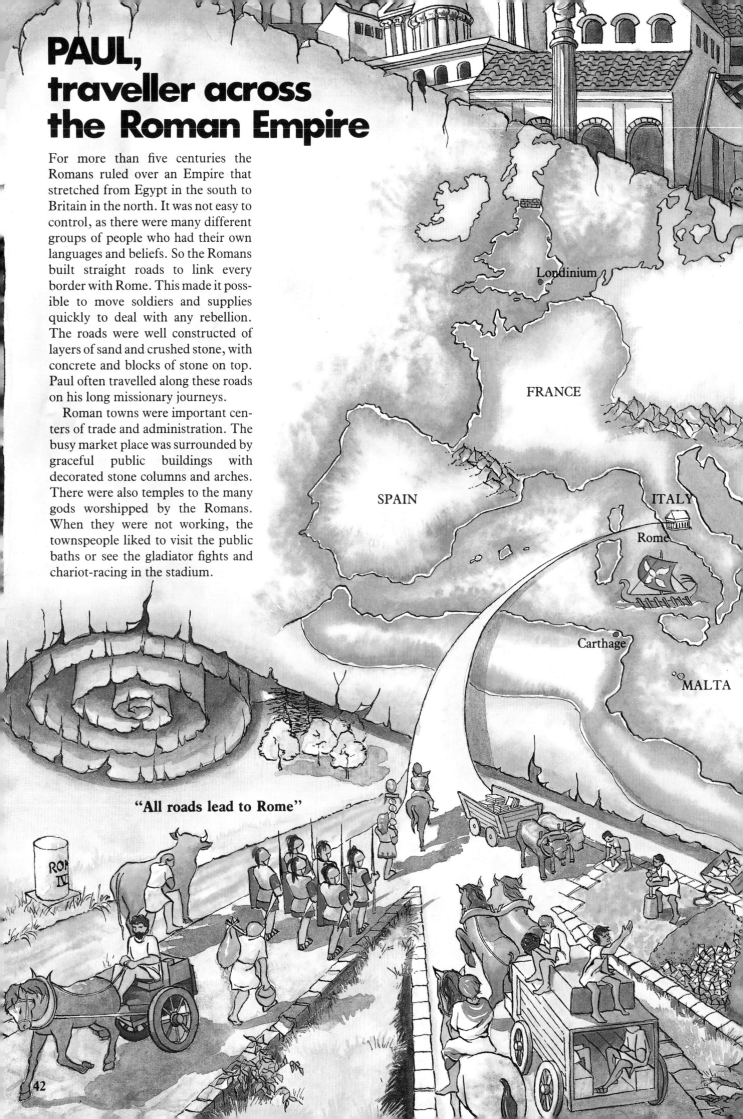

Londinium

FRANCE

SPAIN

ITALY

Rome

Carthage

MALTA

"All roads lead to Rome"

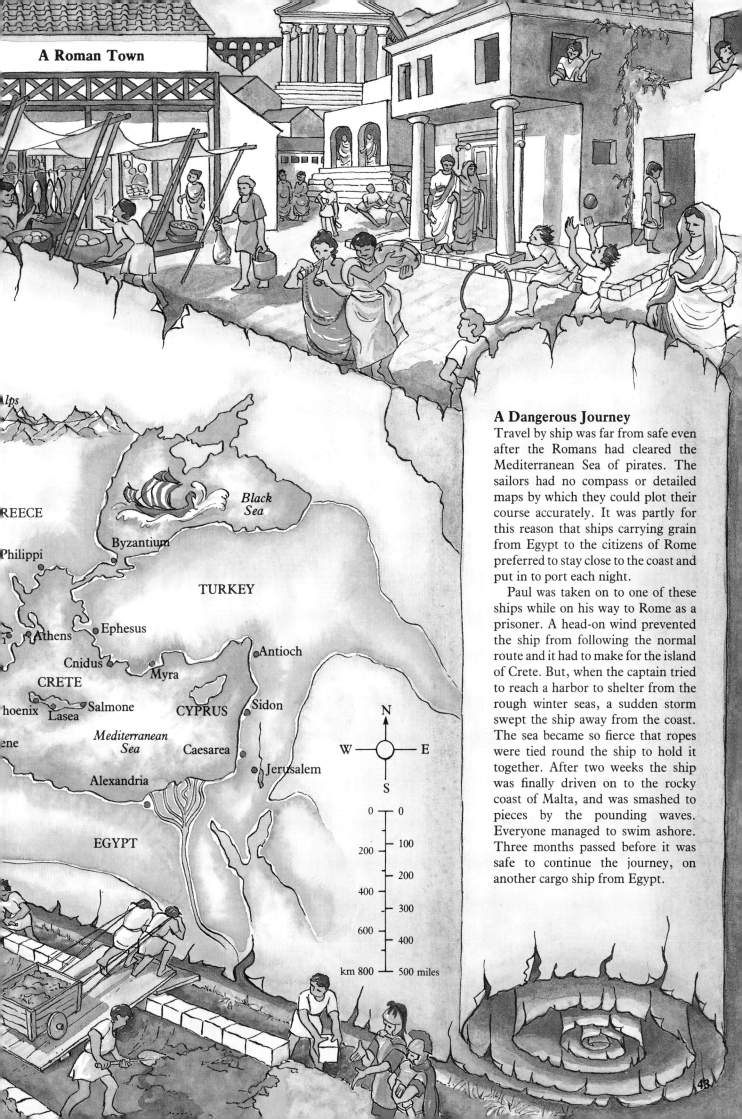

A Roman Town

A Dangerous Journey

Travel by ship was far from safe even after the Romans had cleared the Mediterranean Sea of pirates. The sailors had no compass or detailed maps by which they could plot their course accurately. It was partly for this reason that ships carrying grain from Egypt to the citizens of Rome preferred to stay close to the coast and put in to port each night.

Paul was taken on to one of these ships while on his way to Rome as a prisoner. A head-on wind prevented the ship from following the normal route and it had to make for the island of Crete. But, when the captain tried to reach a harbor to shelter from the rough winter seas, a sudden storm swept the ship away from the coast. The sea became so fierce that ropes were tied round the ship to hold it together. After two weeks the ship was finally driven on to the rocky coast of Malta, and was smashed to pieces by the pounding waves. Everyone managed to swim ashore. Three months passed before it was safe to continue the journey, on another cargo ship from Egypt.

Alps

GREECE

Black Sea

Byzantium

Philippi

TURKEY

Athens · Ephesus

Cnidus

Antioch

Myra

CRETE

Phoenix · Lasea · Salmone

CYPRUS

Sidon

ene

Mediterranean Sea

Caesarea

Jerusalem

Alexandria

EGYPT

N
W — E
S

km	miles
0	0
200	100
400	200
600	300
	400
km 800	500 miles

A Roman harbor

Like other civilian passengers, Paul had to travel across the Mediterranean Sea in the cramped quarters of cargo boats. Steered by two oar-like rudders, these boats were driven forward by the wind as it filled the large square mainsail.

When Paul reached the safety of a busy harbor he could watch the wooden cranes creak into position and transfer cargo to the waiting carts. Roman galleys, or warships, moved swiftly past with lines of brightly colored shields glinting in the sun. The long spike of the corvus might be a good perch for seagulls, but in battle it could be lowered on to an enemy boat, locking the two together. Soldiers were then able to storm across the bridge. At other times the enemy was rammed by the boat's pointed bow. Paul knew that galleys did not depend on the wind alone for their speed; a hundred or more slaves were chained to benches below deck and forced to pull heavy oars in time to the beat of a drum.

Jacob Genesis chapter 25, verses 19–23

Moses Exodus chapter 5, verses 1–21

Deborah Judges chapter 4, verses 4–16

Ruth Ruth chapter 2, verses 1–13 and chapter 4, verses 1–22

Solomon 1 Kings chapter 10, verses 1–29

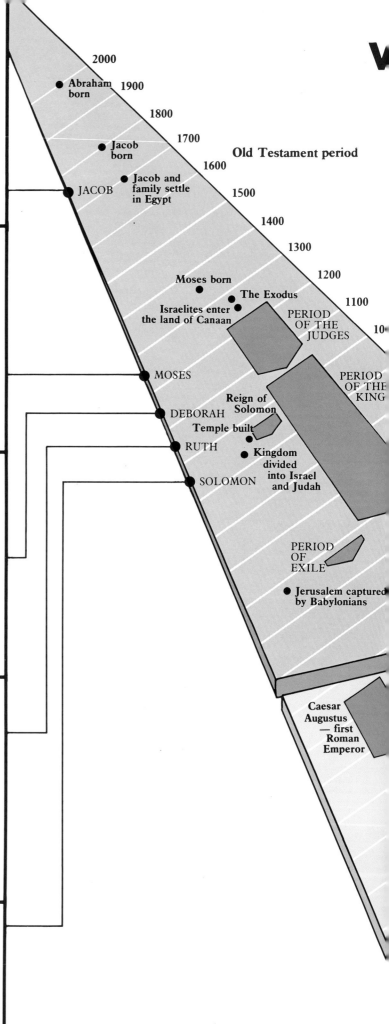

2000

● Abraham born 1900

1800

● Jacob born 1700

1600

JACOB ● Jacob and family settle in Egypt

Old Testament period

1500

1400

1300

● Moses born

● The Exodus 1200

● Israelites enter the land of Canaan

1100

PERIOD OF THE JUDGES

10

MOSES

DEBORAH Reign of Solomon

PERIOD OF THE KING

Temple built

RUTH ● Kingdom divided into Israel and Judah

SOLOMON

PERIOD OF EXILE

● Jerusalem captured by Babylonians

Caesar Augustus — first Roman Emperor

? WHERE? WHEN?

Jeremiah Jeremiah chapter 27, verses 1–11 and chapter 28, verses 10–17

Where can I find these people in the Bible?
The drawings link back to the stories in this book and the Bible references show where to find these stories in the Bible.

When did these people live?
The time chart shows when these people lived. Some of the dates are not known exactly. The chart also places important events connected with Bible history.

Esther Esther chapter 5, verses 1–8

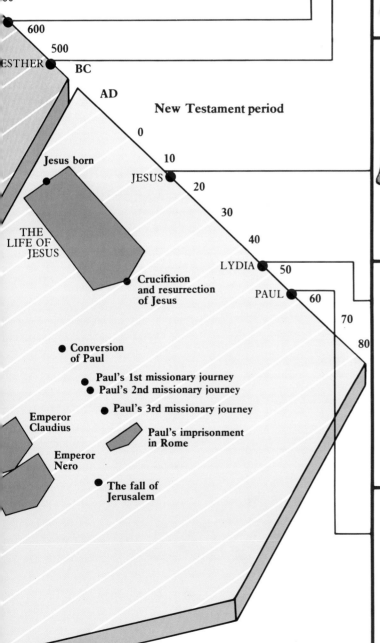

00

600

500

ESTHER

BC

AD

New Testament period

0

Jesus born

JESUS

10

20

30

THE LIFE OF JESUS

40

LYDIA

50

Crucifixion and resurrection of Jesus

PAUL

60

70

80

Conversion of Paul

Paul's 1st missionary journey
Paul's 2nd missionary journey

Paul's 3rd missionary journey

Emperor Claudius

Paul's imprisonment in Rome

Emperor Nero

The fall of Jerusalem

Jesus Mark chapter 3, verses 1–6

Lydia Acts chapter 16, verses 11–15

47

Paul Acts chapter 27

Index to main topics covered in the book